Igniting Excellence through Empathy

By

Tara Ferrell

First Printing, 2023

The website address is: www.taraferrell.com

The Manifesting Lifestyle, LLC

Tara Ferrell asserts the moral right to be identified as the author of this work.

Igniting Excellence through Empathy

Chapter 1

Understanding the Power of Empathy in Leadership

Empathy, at its core, is the ability to understand and share the feelings, experiences, and perspectives of others. It involves stepping into someone else's shoes, seeing the world from their vantage point, and connecting with them on an emotional level. Empathy in leadership means being able to relate to and genuinely care about the well-being and success of team members.

In the context of leadership, empathy plays a vital role in building strong relationships, and creating a positive work environment. It goes beyond sympathy or pity, as it requires actively engaging with others and seeking to understand their emotions and experiences.

Empathy in leadership is crucial because it acknowledges the human element within the workplace. It recognizes that individuals are not just cogs in a machine but complex beings with their own struggles and motivations.

When leaders demonstrate empathy, they create a sense of psychological safety, where team members feel comfortable expressing their thoughts, concerns, and ideas. This psychological safety encourages open communication and cooperation. Employees are more likely to go the extra mile when they feel that their leaders genuinely care about their well-being.

Empathy allows leaders to tailor their approach to meet the unique needs of each individual. By understanding their team members' perspectives and challenges, leaders can provide appropriate support and guidance.

This understanding empowers leaders to fine-tune their communication and motivational strategies, creating a sense of inclusivity and belonging among their team.

Furthermore, empathy allows leaders to anticipate potential roadblocks or areas of concern for each team member. By comprehending the challenges and expectations unique to individuals, leaders can proactively address obstacles and provide guidance that not only ensures personal growth but also contributes to the overall success of the team and the organization.

Consider, for example, a scenario involving a team member who is going through personal difficulties, such as a loss in their family. One day they receive devastating news of the sudden passing of their father. Their team leader immediately senses that they need support during this challenging time. Instead of pushing them to continue working as usual, the leader schedules a private meeting with the employee to discuss their concerns.

An effective leader understands that the employee might need some time off to be with their family and attend the funeral. They also assure the employee that the team will cover their workload and extend their full support during the absence.

The team leader informs the employee about bereavement leave options and other resources available to help them cope with the situation. The leader establishes a link between the employee and the company's employee assistance program, a resource offering counseling services to individuals with personal challenges.

Throughout the following weeks, the leader regularly checks in on the employee to see how they are doing. They are considerate and accommodating, adjusting the employee's workload and deadlines as needed to reduce any additional stress. The team leader also encourages other team members to lend a hand, ensuring a positive and supportive atmosphere in the workplace.

By demonstrating genuine concern for their team member's well-being, the team leader not only supported the employee during the difficult time but also promoted a culture of compassion within the team.

As a result of the leader's understanding the team member feels a sense of support and comfort. They recognize that their leader truly cares about their well-being and understands the difficulties they are facing. This creates a strong bond of trust between the team member and the leader, as they feel valued and supported during a vulnerable time in their life.

This type of leadership nurtures an employee-supportive environment. By creating trust, leaders create a space where employees feel comfortable taking risks and sharing unconventional ideas. As a result, the employees feel confident that their contributions will be appreciated and respected, regardless of the outcome.

The embodiment of empathetic leadership is vividly demonstrated by Yvon Chouinard, the founder of Patagonia, who serves as a prime example of empathetic leadership in action.

Chouinard's emphasis on work-life balance has not only earned Patagonia a reputation as a socially responsible company but has also created a culture where employees thrive.

Chouinard's approach to leadership is reflected in the company's policies and practices. For instance, Patagonia offers flexible work hours, allowing employees to maintain a healthy work-life balance. This understanding reflects Chouinard's recognition of the diverse needs and challenges faced by employees, such as caring for children or addressing family obligations.

By offering flexible work hours, Patagonia acknowledges that employees have responsibilities and commitments outside of work. Flexibility empowers employees to manage their time effectively, reducing stress and allowing them to be more present and engaged when they are at work.

Another example of Patagonia's empathetic policies is their provision of on-site childcare facilities. This initiative demonstrates understanding of the challenges faced by working parents and the importance of supporting them in balancing their professional and personal responsibilities. By offering on-site childcare, Patagonia removes barriers that working parents often face, providing a convenient and supportive environment for their children while they work.

The provision of on-site childcare not only supports working parents but also creates a sense of community and family-friendly atmosphere within the organization. It allows employees to feel more at ease and focused on their work, knowing that their children are in a safe and nurturing environment nearby.

These policies and practices are a testament to Chouinard's empathetic leadership style. They demonstrate his genuine concern for the diverse needs and challenges of employees.

Empathetic leaders wield a remarkable and transformative influence within organizations, leaving a lasting mark by crafting work environments that radiate positivity and driving innovation and success through a compassionate lens. Their unique approach to leadership centers around a commitment to their employees' well-being. This intentional focus encourages an atmosphere where employees feel not only valued but also empowered to contribute their best.

As a result, their teams are inspired to reach new heights of achievement. This emotional investment translates into exceptional dedication and a willingness to go the extra mile to realize organizational goals.

Team Building Goals

Team-Building Goals:

- **Goal:**
  - Brief description of the team-building goal you want to achieve.
  - Why is this goal important for the team's success and cohesion?

- **Action Steps:**
  - List specific actions or strategies you'll implement to achieve this goal.
  - Assign responsibilities if applicable.

- **Timeline:**
  - Estimate when you plan to accomplish each action step.
  - Indicate the completion date for the overall goal.

- **Progress:**
  - Regularly update this section to track your progress toward achieving the goal.
  - Note any challenges encountered and how you addressed them.

Reflection and Adaptation:

Reflect on the progress you've made as a team in achieving these goals:
- What positive changes have you noticed within the team since setting these goals?

- Are there any adjustments needed to your action plans or timelines?
- How have these team-building efforts contributed to improved collaboration and communication?

Next Steps:

Based on your reflections, determine your next steps:
- Are there any goals that need further refinement or adjustments?
- What additional goals or activities should you consider for future team-building efforts?
- How will you continue to prioritize and integrate team-building into your regular operations?

How Will Empathy Effect My

Team?

PROS	CONS

Chapter 2

Developing Self-Awareness and Emotional

Intelligence

Exploring self-awareness as a foundation for leadership involves delving into the complexities of our emotions and thoughts. Through self-awareness, leaders gain insights into how their own emotions shape their behaviors and interactions with others. This understanding allows them to navigate their emotions in a way that promotes compassion and positive connections with their team members.

The practice of self-awareness furnishes leaders with an understanding of their emotional triggers and biases. This heightened awareness permits leaders to address potential challenges before they escalate. By acknowledging their own vulnerabilities and triggers, leaders are better positioned to approach interactions with empathy and genuine understanding.

For example, let's consider a leader who recognizes the impact of stress on their behavior. They become aware that when under stress, they tend to become more controlling or impatient with their team members. Armed with this new self-awareness, the leader can take proactive measures to manage their stress levels and prevent it from negatively affecting their relationships.

The leader might adopt stress-management techniques such as mindfulness exercises or physical activities to mitigate the impact of stress. They might also communicate with their team about the stressors they are experiencing, fostering open and honest dialogue.

Self-aware leaders engage in regular reflection, taking time to evaluate the impact of their emotions on their team dynamics. They consider how their emotional state affects the team's morale and overall performance.

Recognizing strengths and areas for improvement as a leader is a fundamental component of developing strong leadership skills. By understanding their strengths, leaders can use them in a way that increases their impact and contributes to their effectiveness.

For instance, a successful leader might identify strengths such as strong communication skills, strategic thinking, or the ability to inspire and motivate others. They are aware of how these strengths positively influence their ability to connect with their team. They recognize that their communication skills enable them to share their vision and inspire their team members to achieve their best results.

In addition to identifying strengths, leaders also acknowledge their areas for growth. They have the humility to recognize that there is always room for improvement and are open to continuous learning. They invest time and effort into personal and professional development activities such as attending workshops, training programs, reading books, seeking coaching or mentorship programs. They actively work on acquiring new skills and expanding their knowledge base.

Leaders seek feedback from their team members and others, valuing different perspectives and insights. They welcome constructive criticism as an opportunity for growth and self-improvement. By embracing feedback, they gain an understanding of how their emotions and behaviors impact those around them, allowing for correction and adjustments. This heightened emotional intelligence is essential for effective leadership.

Emotional intelligence involves the ability to understand and manage emotions both within oneself and in others. Leaders with high emotional intelligence possess the skills to accurately perceive and interpret emotions, enabling them to respond empathetically and appropriately in various situations.

For example, imagine a manager who leads a team of sales representatives. The manager is known for their high emotional intelligence, which allows them to accurately perceive and interpret emotions in their team members.

One day, one of the managers team members seems visibly upset and withdrawn during a team meeting. Instead of ignoring their behavior or assuming they are just having a bad day, the manager senses that something might be bothering the team member. After the meeting, the manager approaches them with concern and asks if they are okay.

The team member opens up and shares that they have been dealing with personal challenges lately, affecting their performance and mood at work. The manager listens to the team members' concerns and reassures them that it's okay to have difficult times. By actively listening, the manager creates a safe space for the team member to express their emotions without fear of judgment.

After their conversation, the manager recognizes the need to offer support to the team member during this tough time. The manager adjusts the team members workload temporarily, allowing them some breathing room to deal with their personal matters.

A leader is attuned to the emotional cues and signals of their team members. They can recognize subtle signs of frustration, disengagement, or enthusiasm. By being aware of these emotions, they gain insights into the underlying causes and motivations driving their team's behaviors.

For example, let's consider a leader who notices one of their team members displaying signs of frustration during a project. Instead of brushing off or dismissing these emotions, the leader takes steps to address the situation.

Firstly, the leader actively engages with the individual, expressing concern and interest. They approach the team member in a supportive and non-judgmental manner, creating a safe space for open communication. This allows the team member to feel comfortable expressing their frustrations and concerns without fear of retribution.

The leader listens attentively, giving their full presence to the conversation. They pay close attention not only to the words being spoken but also to the emotions and non-verbal cues being displayed. By doing so, the leader validates the team member's feelings, acknowledging the significance of their frustrations and recognizing their impact on their well-being and work performance.

During the conversation, the successful leader seeks to understand the root cause of the team member's frustration. They ask open-ended questions and encourage the team member to share their perspective, allowing them to express their thoughts and concerns fully. The leader refrains from making assumptions or jumping to conclusions, focusing instead on active listening.

By engaging with the individual, the leader shows their commitment to addressing the issues rather than simply brushing them aside. This fosters a sense of trust and openness within the team, encouraging others to feel comfortable sharing their own challenges and seeking support when needed.

Following this conversation, the perceptive leader takes appropriate actions based on the insights gained. They may offer guidance or resources to help lessen the team member's frustrations. Additionally, the leader explores ways to improve the work process or adjust responsibilities to prevent similar issues from arising in the future.

By addressing the emotions in a supportive and understanding manner, the leader can help the team member navigate the challenges they are facing. The empathetic leader recognizes that emotions significantly impact team dynamics and individual performance, and by addressing them proactively, they cultivate a more positive and productive work environment.

An empathetic leader possesses advanced skills in managing their own emotions. They recognize the importance of self-regulation and have developed the ability to keep their emotions in check, particularly during high-pressure situations. They understand that their emotional state can influence their decision-making and overall leadership effectiveness.

A leader recognizes that their reactions and behaviors can influence the emotional climate within the team. Therefore, they make a conscious effort to model emotional regulation and display a positive attitude, even in the face of adversity.

Consider a publishing company which specializes in producing both print and digital books. The company is undergoing a major restructuring due to shifts in the industry and changes in consumer preferences. As a result, there's a sense of uncertainty and apprehension among the employees.

The leader of the company is known for their ability to navigate challenging situations with empathy and composure. One day, during a company-wide meeting, the leader addresses the concerns head-on. Instead of glossing over the changes or downplaying the challenges, they acknowledge the employees' concerns.

Recognizing that open communication is vital, the leader of the company invites employees to share their thoughts and ideas openly. In response to concerns about job security, the leader provides insights into the company's strategic plans and the steps being taken to ensure a smooth transition including retraining programs, opportunities for cross-functional collaboration and the creation of new roles in the company.

As a result of the company's leadership, the publishing company undergoes a successful adaptation to the evolving industry landscape. The team remains motivated and unified, driven by the leader's ability to channel emotions positively and effectively.

As illustrated in these examples, during challenging circumstances, an effective leader consciously chooses a constructive and empathetic approach. Instead of allowing negative emotions like anger, frustration, or anxiety to drive their actions, they draw upon their emotional intelligence to respond in a manner that promotes understanding and resolution.

For example, when faced with a conflict within the team, an emotionally intelligent leader maintains composure and refrains from becoming defensive or aggressive. By regulating their own emotions, they avoid personal attacks or blame, focusing instead on finding common ground and facilitating effective communication among team members.

Emotional regulation techniques, such as deep breathing exercises or taking breaks, help in managing and controlling emotions during challenging situations

Journaling provides a space for leaders to explore and document their inner world. Through regular journaling, leaders can gain insights into their patterns of thinking and emotional responses. They can examine their decision-making processes and track their personal growth in developing leadership skills.

Mindfulness practices, such as meditation and mindful breathing, encourage present-moment awareness and non-judgmental observation of one's thoughts. It helps successful leaders recognize and understand their emotions as they arise, enabling them to respond effectively.

By incorporating reflective practices like journaling and mindfulness into their routine, leaders create space for self-reflection and deep understanding. This empowers leaders to pause, observe, and purposefully decide how to respond to situations, particularly in moments infused with strong emotions.

Engaging in self-assessment exercises, such as personality assessments or emotional intelligence assessments, further deepens leaders' understanding of themselves and their emotional intelligence. These assessments provide tools to evaluate their strengths and areas for development.

Developing self-awareness and emotional intelligence gives leaders the opportunity to overcome their emotional triggers and ingrained biases, thus creating a profound understanding of both oneself and others.

SELF-COMPASSION

What are you criticizing yourself about? _____

_____

_____

What emotions are you feeling? _____

_____

_____

What tone, phrases and words are you using? _____

_____

_____

What would you tell a good friend who is thinking or feeling this way? _____

_____

_____

If you were confronting this voice in a calm, mature manner, what would you say?

_____

_____

How can you view the situation or reframe those thoughts and phrases to one that is kinder and more positive?

_____

_____

_____

In 1 week, 1 month, year or more, how will I feel about this? Does it matter that much? Can I release this now?

_____

_____

_____

DECLUTTER YOUR MIND

Our minds are filled with clutter. Just as a cluttered home can be decluttered, so can a cluttered mind. Daily stress, poor mental habits, and unfinished business are a few of the causes of mental clutter.

Answer these questions to gain insight toward reducing your mental clutter:

1. What are the excess items in my home and work environment that contribute to my mental clutter?

2. Are there unnecessary people in my life that create additional clutter? Who are they? How can I lessen their impact?

3. How do I distract myself? What do I do when I procrastinate?

DECLUTTER YOUR MIND

4. When can I implement focused breathing into my routine?

5. How can I add at least one 20-minute daily meditation session into my life?

6. How would my life change if I were able to reduce my mental clutter by at least 50 percent?

7. What are the negative thoughts I experience regularly? How do these impact the rest of my day?

Right now...

What do you do to relax when you're
feeling stressed or anxious?

_____

_____

_____

_____

_____

_____

_____

_____

_____

_____

_____

_____

_____

_____

_____

_____

_____

Right now...

What kind of things are likely to affect your
stress and anxiety levels?

_____

_____

_____

_____

_____

_____

_____

_____

_____

_____

_____

_____

_____

_____

_____

_____

_____

_____

Try new things...

Make a list of things you'd like to try to
help you relax

- [ ]
- [ ]
- [ ]
- [ ]
- [ ]
- [ ]
- [ ]
- [ ]
- [ ]
- [ ]
- [ ]
- [ ]
- [ ]
- [ ]
- [ ]
- [ ]
- [ ]
- [ ]
- [ ]
- [ ]

Try This...

Take 15 minutes out to sit in nature and observe
your surroundings. Write about how this feels.

Try This...

Listen to some calming music, really focusing on the
sounds. Write about how this feels.

_____

_____

_____

_____

_____

_____

_____

_____

_____

_____

_____

_____

_____

_____

_____

_____

_____

_____

_____

Chapter 3

Cultivating a Culture of Trust and Psychological Safety

Trust and psychological safety are crucial elements in fostering a positive work environment. They play a fundamental role in promoting employee well-being, engagement, and overall organizational success. Trust builds strong relationships and enables effective collaboration, while psychological safety creates an environment where individuals feel safe to express their opinions and voice concerns without fear of negative consequences.

When trust and psychological safety are present, employees experience higher job satisfaction, commitment, and motivation. Leaders play a pivotal role in cultivating trust and psychological safety in the workplace.

Emotional well-being is a critical factor that contributes to increased employee engagement, as individuals who feel psychologically safe are more likely to actively participate and contribute to their work. When employees feel secure in expressing their ideas and opinions without fear of judgment or negative repercussions, they are more willing to take risks and think outside the box.

First and foremost, leaders should set the tone by demonstrating transparent and receptive behavior themselves. This can involve sharing their own thoughts, challenges, and vulnerabilities, demonstrating that open expression is both welcomed and valued.

Active listening becomes a cornerstone of this approach, with leaders dedicating time and attention to genuinely hear and understand the perspectives of their team members.

Additionally, empowering team members in decision-making processes further instills a sense of ownership and trust, bolstering their confidence to share thoughts openly. Conflict resolution mechanisms play a critical role as well, assuring individuals that any disputes will be addressed fairly and impartially. To create a truly safe space, confidentiality should be upheld, allowing team members to share without fear of repercussions.

Regular one-on-one check-ins provide a private avenue for team members to express concerns or ideas, strengthening a deeper sense of connection. An open-door policy, coupled with various channels for feedback, such as suggestion boxes or anonymous surveys, ensures that multiple avenues for communication are available.

Effective leaders play a pivotal role in cultivating an atmosphere of respect and inclusion. By encouraging a culture where every individual is valued and their contributions are acknowledged, leaders create conditions that embraces diversity and create space for everyone's voice to be heard.

Leaders are also responsible for reinforcing respectful behavior, setting the tone for the organization. They can lead by example by actively seeking and considering different perspectives and addressing any instances of disrespectful behavior promptly and effectively.

Imagine a CEO who leads a growing technology company. This CEO believes that as a leader, they play a crucial role in encouraging open discussions in the organization. They actively seek and consider varying perspectives from employees at all levels of the organization. When a decision needs to be made, they make sure to involve relevant team members with different backgrounds and experiences to ensure a well-rounded and comprehensive decision-making process.

One day, during a project review meeting, tensions rise between two team members. One member dismisses the ideas of the other without giving them fair consideration. Recognizing the situation as a potential instance of disrespectful behavior, the CEO intervenes. The leader addresses the issue calmly but firmly, reminding both members about the importance of valuing each other's contributions and maintaining a respectful work environment.

In private, the CEO speaks separately with both individuals. The leader listens to both teammates perspectives and provides constructive feedback on how their actions could impact team dynamics. Additionally, the CEO emphasizes the importance of empathy and understanding when working together. By addressing the situation promptly and openly, the CEO sends a clear message that disrespectful behavior is not tolerated within the organization.

Furthermore, the CEO ensures that the company's policies and code of conduct reflect the values of respect and inclusion. The leader regularly communicates these values through company-wide emails, town hall meetings, and team gatherings. They take the time to recognize and celebrate instances of respectful behavior and teamwork, reinforcing the importance of these behaviors within the company culture.

Integrity is another vital component of building trust. Leaders who consistently act with integrity demonstrate ethical behavior, honesty, and consistency in their actions and words. They keep their promises, admit mistakes, and take responsibility for their actions.

By modeling integrity, leaders inspire trust and set an example for others to follow.

Transparency is a crucial aspect of trust-building. When leaders are transparent in their decision-making processes and communication it promotes an environment of openness and honesty. Transparent leaders provide clarity and avoid hidden agendas. This transparency creates trust among team members as they feel informed and included in the organization's direction and decision-making.

Open communication is a key enabler of trust-building. When leaders support an environment of open communication, it encourages individuals to express their opinions and concerns freely. Leaders who actively listen create a culture where everyone's voice is heard and respected.

Let's consider another scenario, imagine a team leader, who works in a tech company. During team meetings, the leader shares information about the company's goals, projects, and challenges. They provide updates on important decisions and explain the reasoning behind them. By openly sharing this information, they ensure that their team members feel included and informed, eliminating any doubts or uncertainties. This transparency allows team members to understand the bigger picture and make more informed contributions.

The team leader also believes in the value of two-way communication. They encourage their team members to express their concerns and ideas openly. Whenever possible, they organize feedback sessions and brainstorming meetings where everyone has the opportunity to contribute. By listening and valuing the teams input, the leader creates conditions where team members feel heard and valued.

In addition to transparent communication, an accomplished leader understands the importance of integrity. They consistently align their words with their actions and follow through on their commitments. When they make a promise to their team, they make sure to fulfill it. By demonstrating their integrity, they earn the trust and respect of their team members.

Once again, let's consider a scenario in which a challenging situation arises where a key client requests a last-minute change to a project deliverable. The leaders team works to meet the original deadline, and this change seems nearly impossible. However, the team leader remains true to their commitment of open communication and integrity.

The leader calls an emergency meeting with their team and openly discussed the situation. They acknowledge the difficulty of the request and listen to their teams concerns and ideas. The leader encourages their team members to voice their opinions and explore alternative solutions. Together, they brainstorm potential approaches, weighing the pros and cons of each.

After careful deliberation, the leader makes a decision that aligns with the best interests of both the client and the team. They communicate this decision transparently, explaining the rationale behind it. Despite the challenging circumstances, the leaders team trusts their judgment and remains motivated, knowing that their leader has considered their input.

At the heart of trust and psychological safety within teams and organizations lies effective communication. This essential element not only establishes pathways for valuable feedback but also enables the timely and constructive resolution of concerns. By actively seeking and valuing feedback, leaders show a commitment to improvement and growth.

Let's take the example of a manager working for a software development company. The manager understands the value of open dialogue and active listening in creating trust within the team. The manager believes that creating circumstances where everyone feels comfortable expressing their ideas and concerns is essential for the team's success.

During a team meeting, the manager introduces a new project that requires new solutions and fresh ideas. As the team gathers around the table, the manager sets the stage for open dialogue by emphasizing the importance of each team member's perspective. They encourage the team to share their thoughts and ideas without hesitation.

As the discussion begins, the manager listens to each team member, maintaining eye contact and nodding to show engagement. The manager make sure everyone has the opportunity to speak and express their opinions. The manager makes sure to ask insightful questions, seeking to understand the reasoning behind their suggestions and encouraging further discussion.

One team member has reservations about the proposed approach. They hesitate to voice their concerns, fearing that their ideas might not be well-received. Sensing the team members hesitation, the manager makes a point of specifically asking for the team members input, assuring that every idea is valuable and will be respectfully considered.

Empowered by the managers encouragement, the team member opens up and shares their concerns, offering an alternative perspective then those given by the other teammates. The manager listens and thanks them for bringing their unique insights to the table. The manager acknowledges the validity of their concerns and encourages the team to consider the team members ideas alongside the others.

As the discussion continues, the team engages in a constructive exchange of thoughts, combining different perspectives to shape a more comprehensive approach. The manager facilitates the dialogue, ensuring that the team members respect each other's opinions and remained focused on the common goal.

Through their open dialogue, the team reaches a breakthrough. They devise a strategy that incorporates the best ideas and addresses potential difficulties. The team members feel a sense of ownership and pride, knowing that their contributions are valued and will influence the project's direction.

In the weeks that follow, the team's dynamics transform. Trust grows stronger as team members continue to share their thoughts and concerns openly.

The managers commitment to open dialogue and active listening has an impact on the team's performance and the members appreciate their managers leadership style.

Recognizing the immense value of diversity is important for all leaders. In today's global and interconnected world, leaders recognize that diversity fosters creativity and a deeper understanding of the needs and preferences of their teams and customers.

Successful leaders understand that diversity goes beyond surface-level differences such as race, gender, or ethnicity. It encompasses a broad range of dimensions, including age, background, culture, skills, and perspectives. When team members come from different backgrounds and possess varied experiences, they bring fresh perspectives to problem-solving and decision-making processes.

Leaders who prioritize diversity in their team create a work environment that attracts top talent from all backgrounds. They understand that individuals are more likely to join and stay in organizations that prioritize and recognize the value of diverse perspectives.

Google, a multinational technology company, has gained recognition for its commitment to creating a culture of trust and psychological safety within the organization.

A demonstration of Google's commitment to these initiatives is evident in their renowned "20%

Time" policy. This program allows employees to dedicate 20% of their work hours to pursue projects of personal interest, even if they are unrelated to their current responsibilities. This freedom encourages employees to explore their passions, take risks, and pursue ideas without the fear of failure or negative consequences. The company's trust in its employees creates a psychological safety net that fosters creativity and experimentation.

For example, Google's popular products like Gmail and Google News originated from employees' side projects during their 20% Time. These programs showcase how allowing an environment of openness and confidence in employees can unleash their creative capabilities. Their employees report high levels of job satisfaction and engagement, leading to increased productivity and retention rates. The company has grown a reputation as an employer of choice, attracting top talent from around the world.

Successful leaders play an essential part in upholding psychological safety and trust in the workplace. The connection between trust and feeling safe to express opinions is crucial for business success.

This collaboration not only forms strong connections and promotes open dialogue between leaders and team members but also enhances employee happiness, dedication, and motivation.

HOW DO I CULTIVATE TRUST WITH MY TEAM

Constructive Feedback Guide Sheet

Frame your feedback using "I" statements to express your perspective and feelings to avoid sounding accusatory.

Be Descriptive, Not Judgemental:
Describe what you observed without attaching value judgments. Explain how the behavior affected you or the team.

Be Objective:
Base your feedback on facts and observable behavior rather than assumptions or personal opinions.

Provide Context:
Give context by explaining why the behavior matters and its impact on the team, project, or organization.

Offer Specific Examples:
Back up your feedback with concrete examples that illustrate the behavior you are discussing.

Balance Positive and Negative Feedback:
Start with positive aspects (if applicable) before addressing areas that need improvement. This creates a more balanced and receptive atmosphere.

Suggest Solutions:
If appropriate, offer suggestions for improvement or alternative approaches to the behavior in question.

Encourage Two-Way Communication:
Create an environment where the recipient feels comfortable discussing their perspective. Encourage questions and clarifications.

Ask For Their Perspective:
Inquire about their thoughts on the feedback and how they perceive the situation. This can lead to a more open dialog.

Listen Actively:
Pay attention to their response and listen without interruption. Show that you value their input.

Focus on Growth and Improvement:
Emphasize that the goal of the feedback is to help develop and succeed, not to criticize or blame.

Use Positive Language:
Frame feedback in a positive and encouraging manner. Highlight their strengths and potential for growth.

Be Patient and Supportive:
Understand that change takes time. Offer your support and willingness to assist in their improvement.

Follow Up:
Check-in at a later time to see how they are progressing and whether they've implemented any changes based on the feedback.

Chapter 4

Fostering Resilience and Well-being

Resilience plays a crucial role in the success and well-being of leaders and team members within organizations. It enables individuals to overcome opposition, adapt to change, and maintain their mental and emotional health in the face of adversity. Recognizing the importance of resilience, organizations are increasingly emphasizing the establishment of a positive work environment that promotes the overall well-being of their employees.

One key aspect of resilience is the ability to overcome challenges and adapt to change. In today's rapidly evolving business landscape, leaders and team members need to navigate unforeseen circumstances, embrace innovation, and find effective solutions. Resilient individuals demonstrate a growth mindset, viewing difficulties as opportunities for growth and learning.

In the midst of this economic turmoil, a manufacturing company found itself particularly vulnerable due to reduced consumer spending and intensified competition. The leadership team of this company recognized the dire need for a transformative strategy to not only weather the storm but to emerge stronger in the face of adversity.

Instead of yielding to the overwhelming challenges, the company's leaders exhibited resilience by adopting a growth mindset. They reframed the seemingly insurmountable obstacles as unique opportunities to reimagine their business direction. This shift prompted the company to pivot from its conventional manufacturing practices and embrace a more forward-thinking approach.

With innovation at the forefront, the company transitioned its focus from traditional manufacturing to pioneering eco-friendly products and sustainable practices. However, this profound change required not only strategic adjustments but also emotional resilience from the employees. The leadership team recognized the importance of supporting and nurturing their employees' emotional well-being during the transition. They implemented training programs, counseling services, and open forums for employees to express their concerns and feelings, promoting a culture of support and understanding.

This bold move not only breathed new life into the company but also positioned it as an industry trailblazer in the realm of environmentally conscious manufacturing. Employee emotional resilience played a pivotal role in propelling the company forward, as a workforce that felt supported and equipped to navigate change contributed to the overall success of the transformation.

As a result of this resilience-driven transformation, the company not only navigated through the economic storm but emerged from it with a newfound strength and relevance.

Nurturing the mental and emotional well-being of employees stands as another vital factor in cultivating resilience. Increasingly, organizations are recognizing that championing the holistic health of their workforce yields heightened engagement and enhanced productivity. Striking a healthy work-life balance becomes instrumental in averting burnout and affording individuals the opportunity to recharge and safeguard their mental well-being.

Consider a dedicated bank manager who is recognized for their strong work ethic and commitment to their team and clients. This manager frequently works beyond regular office hours, to ensure smooth operations of the staff and to meet the changing needs of customers.

As time passes, this manager begins to notice the toll of the demanding schedule on their well-being. Feelings of stress and being overwhelmed become familiar, and they struggled to find time for personal activities and relationships. Concerned friends and family members start to express worries about their health and the amount of time they spend at work away from loved ones.

Recognizing the need for change, the manager decides to prioritize work-life balance. They implement a more structured routine, setting specific start and end times for their workday. Delegating tasks to capable team members becomes a priority, empowering them to take on responsibilities and make decisions independently.

Moreover, the manager makes a conscious effort to disconnect from work-related communication during evenings and weekends. They allocate time for personal interests, family moments, hobbies, and regular exercise.

The results of these changes are significant. The manager experiences higher energy levels, reduced stress, and improved focus when approaching work tasks. The team also thrives, feeling motivated and empowered to assume greater responsibility.

To further enhance this initiative, companies can offer helpful resources and create strong support systems for mental health and overall well-being. For instance, they might provide access to counseling services, set up programs to assist employees, and share useful mental health materials. Think of it like a company setting up a private hotline where employees can get advice and information about different mental health concerns. At the same time, it's important for companies to create a safe and welcoming workplace where people feel comfortable asking for help and talking openly about their mental health struggles.

Resiliency Assessment

Read through the questions below and rate yourself on a scale of 1 to 10. 1 = Not like me at all, 10 = That's me!

	Questions	Score
1.	I have plenty of support from other people	....
2.	I adapt quickly to new developments	....
3.	I'm able to accept myself for who I am	....
4.	I'm able to recover emotionally from losses	....
5.	I feel self-confident and appreciate myself	....
6.	I'm very durable during tough times	....
7.	I'm good at solving problems	....
8.	I'm good at facing challenges	....
9.	I'm good at interacting at times of stress	....
10.	I have found benefits in bad experiences	....

Now add up your overall score ....

What could I do to increase the score?

Chapter 5

Empowering Individuals through Coaching and Mentorship

Coaching and mentorship programs play a pivotal role in nurturing empathetic leadership by encouraging collaborative dynamics and personal growth with leaders and their teams. These programs offer a platform through which leaders can establish meaningful and supportive connections with their team members.

Through engagement in coaching and mentorship initiatives, successful leaders refine their communication and listening skills. Coaching and mentorship experiences encourage leaders to step into the shoes of their team members, offering insight into their unique challenges and personal experiences.

The introspection and self-awareness that often accompany participation in coaching and mentorship programs contribute to individual development. As leaders reflect on their own biases, assumptions, and areas for development, their heightened self-awareness translates into heightened empathy.

Imagine an experienced leader who works with new employees seeking to advance in their careers. The leader uses their expertise and experience to guide the new employees through conversations to help them uncover their true potential. During their first session together, the experienced leader takes the time to understand the new employees' background and career goals. Through thoughtful questioning, the leader encourages the employee to consider their passions and long-term objectives. As the employee shares their experiences and thoughts, the leader listens, providing a safe and supportive space for the employee to open up.

Throughout their coaching sessions, the leader uses their expertise to promote self-awareness in the new employee. The leader helps the employee identify key strengths and talents. Together, they explore how the employees' skills align with their passions and how the employee can leverage unique qualities to pursue a fulfilling career path.

As they progress, the leader guides the employee in setting specific and achievable goals. The leader challenges the employee to step outside their comfort zone and consider new opportunities that align with their career path. With the leaders support, the employee gains clarity and confidence in their decisions, knowing that they are making informed choices based on their true potential.

Additionally, the leader provides the employee with valuable resources, such as networking tips, resume building techniques, and interview strategies. The leader equips the employee with the tools needed to effectively showcase their talents and seize opportunities that align with their newfound clarity and determination.

Through the coaching process with the leader, the employee experiences personal and professional growth. They become more self-assured and focused on their career path, embracing challenges with optimism.

Coaching and mentorship programs empower individuals by supporting a sense of ownership and accountability for their personal and professional development. These programs encourage individuals to set ambitious yet achievable goals, create action plans, and take deliberate steps toward their desired outcomes. By providing a supportive and structured framework, coaching and mentorship programs instill confidence and self-belief in individuals.

Furthermore, coaching and mentorship programs facilitate continuous learning and skill enhancement. They offer individuals the opportunity to acquire new knowledge and refine their abilities through targeted feedback and tailored support.

An excellent illustration of a coaching and mentorship program is run by IBM, a global technology company. They are known for their innovative culture and highly successful mentorship program that empowers individuals to grow and excel in their careers. The program pairs experienced senior leaders with junior employees, creating a valuable opportunity for knowledge sharing and personal development.

In IBM's mentorship program, mentors play a pivotal role in offering guidance and support to their mentees. One significant aspect of IBM's mentorship program is goal setting and action planning.

Mentors collaborate with mentees to set realistic goals. Together, they develop action plans that outline the steps needed to achieve these goals, providing a roadmap for mentees' progress. Regular meetings between mentors and mentees allow for ongoing feedback and evaluation of progress toward these goals.

Furthermore, IBM's mentorship program offers an avenue for expanding professional networks. Mentors, often senior leaders within the company, have extensive networks and can introduce mentees to influential contacts and relevant resources.

The positive outcomes of IBM's mentorship program are reflected in increased employee engagement and higher retention rates. By providing a platform for personal and professional development, IBM demonstrates its commitment to cultivating a culture of growth and learning.

As leaders experience the benefits of empathetic coaching and mentorship, they are more likely to model empathetic behaviors themselves. By leading through example, these leaders demonstrate how to approach difficulties with understanding and consideration.

Furthermore, coaching and mentorship programs equip leaders with conflict resolution and problem-solving skills that consider the emotions and perspectives of all parties involved. As leaders develop an awareness of their own emotions and the emotions of their team through these programs, they are better positioned to foster a workplace that places a high emphasis on collaboration and the well-being of every employee.

Mentorship Coaching

What is your career background?

What are your priorities for your career?

What are you passionate about and how can it help you in your career?

What skills would you like to develop?

What are your strengths and talents?

What is one of the challenges you have been facing at work?

What are your top 3 career goals?

How can I help you?

Chapter 6

Harnessing Empathy for Conflict Resolution and Collaboration

Harnessing empathy is a highly effective and essential approach for conflict resolution and encouraging collaboration in various settings, whether in the workplace, interpersonal relationships, or larger communities.

During conflicts, emotions can run high, and tensions may escalate quickly. However, by understanding and relating to other's perspectives, individuals can create a safe and supportive environment for communication. When people feel understood and listened to, the intensity of emotions tends to de-escalate, allowing for more rational and productive discussions.

Understanding enables individuals to truly grasp the underlying reasons behind the conflict, going beyond the surface-level issues. As a result, parties involved can identify the core concerns and address them in a more meaningful manner. When individuals feel that their feelings and perspectives are acknowledged, they are more willing to cooperate and find common ground.

Imagine a situation where two colleagues are constantly at odds over a project they are collaborating on. Both have strong opinions on how to approach the project, leading to frequent clashes and misunderstandings.

Their manager notices the escalating tension between the two employees and decides to intervene. The manager schedules a private meeting with each of them separately to understand their perspectives and concerns.

During the meeting with the first team member, the leader actively practices empathy, listening attentively to their frustrations and challenges. The team member explains that they feels as if the other employee is not considering their ideas seriously and tends to dismiss their suggestions during team discussions. The team member also shares that they feel undervalued and ignored.

In the second team members meeting, the manager once again employs empathy to gain a deeper understanding of the employee's viewpoint. The employee shares their concerns with the manager, emphasizing their belief that the other team member's approach appears overly risk averse. They express that the suggestions made by the other employee often necessitate significant changes to the project plan, resulting in delays and uncertainty.

After talking with both team members, the manager begins to see the underlying reasons behind the conflict. It becomes evident that their surface-level disagreements stem from their individual insecurities and communication styles. The first team member wants to be acknowledged and respected for their contributions, while the second team member is concerned about the project's efficiency and progress.

Armed with this newfound insight, the manager arranges a joint meeting with both employees. In this meeting, the manager leads the conversation with understanding validating each of their concerns and acknowledging the value they bring to the project.

By addressing the core concerns and emotions behind the conflict, both team members start to see each other's perspectives more clearly. They begin to understand that they both want the project to succeed, albeit in different ways.

With their feelings and perspectives acknowledged, the team members become more open to finding common ground. They collaboratively brainstorm alternative approaches that incorporate both of their ideas, aiming for a balance between innovation and efficiency.

Through this empathetic approach, the manager creates a positive shift in their working relationship. As the colleagues feel more understood and valued, they become willing to cooperate and find solutions together. Over time, their communication improves, and they become a more effective and cohesive team, leading to successful project outcomes.

By actively nurturing compassion, individuals gain the ability to step back from their own viewpoints and appreciate the experiences of others. This broader perspective allows them to identify shared interests and mutual goals, providing a solid foundation for teamwork. It becomes evident that working together towards a shared objective benefits everyone involved rather than engaging in a win-lose mentality.

In the workplace, empathy among team members and leaders can produce a positive and cohesive atmosphere. When conflicts arise, team members can engage in constructive dialogue rather than resorting to blame or confrontation. This approach results in the development of innovative solutions that draw upon the different strengths and perspectives of the team.

Understanding and consideration not only plays a vital role in resolving conflicts between team members but also proves essential in addressing performance issues within the workplace. When dealing with performance challenges, leaders who practice empathy create a supportive and understanding environment for their employees.

Instead of resorting to punitive measures or harsh criticism, leaders take the time to understand the underlying factors affecting an employee's performance. They engage in open conversations, actively listening to the employee's concerns and struggles. By empathizing with the individual's situation, leaders can offer the necessary support and resources to help the employee improve their performance.

Having a broader perspective also helps leaders view performance issues more effectively. Rather than labeling employees as underperformers, they seek to understand potential reasons behind the dip in productivity. This could include personal challenges, lack of training, or a mismatch between the employee's skills and job responsibilities.

For example, let's imagine a manufacturing company, where a supervisor noticed a decline in the performance of a particular production line. Instead of immediately attributing the issue to the workers' lack of dedication, the supervisor decided to approach the situation with compassion and consideration.

The supervisor organized a meeting with the workers on the production line to discuss their concerns and challenges. During the meeting, they encouraged meaningful dialogue and actively listened to the employees' feedback.

Through in-depth conversations, the supervisor learned that the workers were experiencing fatigue and physical strain due to long hours of standing and repetitive tasks. Some employees also mentioned that they felt disconnected from the company's goals and desired more recognition for their hard work.

With this broader perspective gained through empathy, the supervisor recognized that the decline in performance was not solely due to the workers' work ethic but rather a combination of work conditions and morale issues.

To address the concerns, the supervisor implemented several changes. They introduced regular breaks and rotation of tasks to reduce physical strain and fatigue. Additionally, the supervisor organized team-building activities and recognition programs to build a sense of camaraderie and appreciation among the workers.

As a result of the caring and considerate approach, the production line workers felt more valued and supported in their roles. Their motivation and engagement increased, leading to a boost in overall productivity. The improved work conditions and increased team spirit also contributed to a supportive work environment, where workers felt more connected to the company's mission and goals.

Addressing performance issues with empathy enables leaders to develop customized improvement plans that take into account the individual's distinct situation. The focus shifts from a negative approach to one that promotes growth and advancement. Employees sense support and appreciation, fostering heightened motivation and involvement.

Let's consider another example. In a marketing agency, a team leader noticed that one of the employees was struggling to meet performance targets.

Instead of adopting a harsh approach or criticizing the employee's efforts, the team leader decided to approach the situation with consideration.

The team leader scheduled a one-on-one meeting with the employees to discuss their challenges and understand the underlying reasons for their performance issues. During the meeting, the leader listened as the employee shared their concerns. The employee explained that they had been dealing with personal issues outside of work, which had been affecting their focus and energy during office hours.

With this new understanding of the employees' circumstances, the team leader recognized that a tailored improvement plan was needed to support their progress and advancement. The leader acknowledged the personal challenges the employee was facing and assured them that the company would provide the necessary support.

Instead of reprimanding the employee for their performance, the team leader offered flexibility in their work schedule to accommodate their personal needs. They also provided access to counseling services and encouraged the employee to take advantage of resources that could help them cope with the external challenges.

Furthermore, the team leader worked with the employee to set achievable and realistic goals that considered their current circumstances. They offered guidance and mentoring, providing the employee with the tools and support needed to improve their performance gradually.

As a result of this insightful approach, the employee felt supported and valued by their team leader and the organization. Knowing that their challenges were understood and accommodated, they felt more motivated and engaged in their work. The team leader's focus on growth and development rather than punishment created a constructive work environment, encouraging a sense of trust and loyalty between the employee and their leader.

Over time, the employees' performance began to improve, and they were able to meet their targets more consistently. The team leader's empathetic approach transformed the way performance issues were addressed.

When providing feedback, strong leaders consider the employee's feelings and choose words carefully to inspire positive change rather than demoralize. This approach provides a culture of confident and transparent dialogue, where employees feel safe sharing their difficulties and seeking assistance when needed.

Conflict Resolution

Acknowledge the conflict:

Define the issue:

Gather the information:

Generate solutions:

Evaluate and select solutions:

Implement and monitor solutions:

Follow-up and feedback:

4 Stages of Team Building

1 - Forming

This is the phase in which colleagues become acquainted and establish a foundation of trust.

2 - Storming

This is the phase where teams tackle the manner in which they will operate collectively, encompassing aspects of leadership and team dynamics.

3 - Norming

As teams progress beyond the storming stage, members will start recognizing each other's strengths and developing a genuine appreciation for your leadership.

4 - Performing

The ultimate phase of team building marks the period during which teams actively engage in the project, ensuring the team's day-to-day operations run smoothly.

Chapter 7

Building Sustainable and High-Performing Teams

Building sustainable and high-performing teams is paramount for organizations seeking to achieve exceptional results. These teams possess key characteristics such as trust, collaboration, shared goals, effective communication, and conflict resolution. By creating an environment that supports teamwork, organizations can empower their teams to thrive and deliver outstanding outcomes.

High-performing teams exhibit a range of essential characteristics that enable them to excel in their endeavors. One of the key factors is trust, which serves as the cornerstone of their success. Within such teams, members feel safe and supported to express their ideas, opinions, and concerns openly. This atmosphere of trust allows team members to leverage their diverse skills and knowledge towards a common purpose. Shared goals further strengthen the team's unity, providing a clear direction and creating a shared sense of purpose and commitment among all members.

For example, within successful factory setup, trust forms a critical foundation for the success of its production team. The team members feel safe and supported to voice their concerns and suggestions openly on the factory floor. During daily team huddles, employees engage in discussions that encourage an environment of sharing. They freely give ideas for potential improvements to the production process, ranging from optimizing workflows to suggesting better equipment maintenance practices.

This culture of open communication empowers the team to work together to address any production bottlenecks or quality issues that may arise. By encouraging everyone's input, the team taps into different perspectives and experiences. As a result, they can identify and resolve challenges more effectively.

The trust among team members also inspires a sense of camaraderie. Employees willingly offer their expertise and support to their colleagues, even across different departments or roles. This spirit of collaboration allows them to work seamlessly together, sharing knowledge and skills to overcome any obstacles that may impede production.

Additionally, this level of trust and teamwork leads to a more agile workforce. Team members are willing to cross-train in different areas, allowing the company to adapt quickly to changing demands or unforeseen events. This flexibility ensures that production targets are consistently met with exceptional quality standards, even during challenging times.

The emphasis on trust and open communication within the manufacturing company's production team not only enhances their performance but also strengthens their unity as a cohesive and efficient unit. By promoting an environment where everyone's input is valued, the company capitalizes on the collective intelligence and creativity of its team members.

Effective communication is another hallmark of high-performing teams. Team members actively engage in listening to one another, ensuring that ideas and information are conveyed clearly and understood by all. They readily share their thoughts, perspectives, and knowledge, fostering transparency and inclusivity throughout the team. Through effective communication, team members can synchronize their efforts, align their expectations, and make well-informed decisions that benefit the entire group.

High-performing teams also demonstrate strong conflict resolution skills. Rather than avoiding conflicts, they address them promptly and constructively. In times of conflict, team members seek to understand the underlying causes and work collaboratively towards mutually satisfactory solutions. Respectful dialogue, active listening, and a focus on finding win-win outcomes characterize the conflict resolution process, emphasizing the preservation of relationships and promoting personal and professional growth.

Furthermore, high-performing teams value diversity and inclusivity. They recognize and embrace the unique strengths, perspectives, and experiences that each team member brings to the table. This diversity enhances the team's problem-solving capabilities, stimulates innovation, and leads to more robust decision-making.

Creating an environment that supports teamwork and synergy involves several important aspects. One key element is establishing clear roles and responsibilities within the team. By defining each team member's specific tasks, areas of expertise, and decision-making authority, confusion is minimized, and accountability is promoted. This clarity enables efficient collaboration, as team members understand their responsibilities and can work together without duplicating efforts. Moreover, clear roles help team members recognize their unique contributions to the team, creating a sense of purpose and ownership.

For instance, in a sales team, clear roles and responsibilities could involve designating individuals responsible for market research, content creation, social media management, and campaign analysis. Each team member understands their role, the specific tasks they are accountable for, and how their work contributes to the team's overall sales strategy.

Another crucial aspect is encouraging shared accountability among team members. Shared accountability means that all team members collectively take ownership of the team's success and are responsible for delivering on their commitments. This approach supports a sense of trust and reliability within the team. When team members are accountable to one another, they are more likely to support each other and strive for excellence.

Celebrating achievements also plays a vital role in creating a positive team culture. Recognizing and celebrating individual and collective accomplishments boosts morale, reinforces the value of collaboration, and motivates team members to continue performing at their best. Celebrations can take various forms, such as team acknowledgments, public recognition, rewards, or team-building activities. By celebrating achievements, teams create a culture of appreciation, unity, and continuous improvement.

For instance, in a project management team, the recognition system is carefully designed to celebrate achievements in various ways, catering to the preferences and strengths of individual team members.

Team leaders ensure that recognition is not limited to just the completion of major milestones but extends to acknowledge the dedication and hard work put forth by team members on a day-to-day basis.

Public acknowledgment during team meetings serves as a powerful tool to highlight exceptional contributions. Team leaders and colleagues take the opportunity to praise specific individuals for their outstanding efforts and problem-solving skills. This public recognition not only boosts the morale of the recognized team member but also inspires others to excel in their respective roles.

Additionally, the team implements a peer-to-peer recognition program, where team members are encouraged to nominate their colleagues for outstanding performance. This mechanism allows team members to show appreciation for their peers' support, creativity, or willingness to go the extra mile.

Furthermore, the project management team organizes quarterly or annual recognition events, where exceptional achievements are celebrated on a larger scale. During these events, team members receive awards, certificates, or other tangible tokens of appreciation, further underscoring the importance of their contributions to the team's success.

The team also utilizes internal communication channels, such as emails, newsletters, or dedicated recognition boards, to share success stories and highlight individual achievements. This widespread recognition not only boosts team morale but also strengthens the team's sense of unity and camaraderie.

By regularly celebrating achievements and showcasing the value of each team member's contributions, the team advances a positive and motivating work environment, encouraging all members to strive for excellence and work collaboratively towards project success.

By fostering an atmosphere that nurtures collaboration and synergy, organizations empower their teams to excel and build sustainable high-performing units. The role of empathetic leadership is paramount in providing the necessary support and empowerment for teams to achieve exceptional results.

Trust Building Game - Shared Responsibility

Trustor's Task:

- Choose a task that requires collaboration and contribution from both partners. For example, building a tower with building blocks, solving a puzzle, or creating a joint artwork.

- Work together with your partner to complete the chosen task. Actively contribute ideas, effort, and coordination.

- Aim to ensure that both partners have an equal role in the task, maintaining a sense of shared responsibility.

Reflect on:

- Ensuring Shared Responsibility:
    - Describe how you ensured that both partners contributed equally to the task.
    - Did you establish a plan or strategy to distribute responsibilities?
    - How did you communicate to make sure both partners felt valued and involved?
- Managing Disagreements or Differences:
    - Did you encounter any differences of opinion or disagreements during the task?

- How did you handle these challenges while maintaining a sense of collaboration and respect?
- Did you compromise or find common ground? If so, how?

- **Strengthening Trust:**
  - How did this experience of working closely together impact your trust in each other?
  - Did you feel more connected and confident in your partner's abilities?
  - Reflect on how shared responsibility and collaboration influenced your perception of trust within the team.

Optional Variation: For an added layer of challenge, you can introduce a time limit for the task, encouraging partners to work efficiently while maintaining effective communication and collaboration.

Chapter 8

Aligning Values and Purpose for Collective Success

Establishing alignment between values and purpose remains a cornerstone of effective leadership. Foremost, it nurtures a sense of importance and direction among individuals, offering them a clear understanding of the significance of their roles and their direct impact on the organization's overarching goals. This pairing becomes even more potent within the context of empathetic leadership, where leaders forge authentic connections with their team members.

For example, a leader in a healthcare organization may emphasize the value of compassion and the purpose of improving patient well-being. This alignment of values and results inspires healthcare professionals to go the extra mile in providing quality care, as they understand the impact their work has on patients' lives.

Secondly, aligning principles and goals acts as a guiding force for decision-making and actions. When leaders and employees share a common set of values and a clear purpose, it becomes easier to make choices that are in line with the organization's core principles.

For instance, a leader in an environmental conservation nonprofit may prioritize sustainability as a core value and the purpose of preserving natural resources. This alignment guides decision-making, such as implementing eco-friendly practices in the organization's operations and advocating for sustainable policies.

Creating a shared vision and mission statement for the organization plays a crucial role in aligning values and intentions. By involving employees in shaping the vision and values, leaders create a sense of ownership and commitment among the workforce.

For example, a leader in a catering company may conduct brainstorming sessions and gather input from employees to shape the vision of the industry through innovative solutions. This team approach ensures that the shared vision reflects the goals and values of the entire team.

Furthermore, effective communication and consistent reinforcement of the organization's purpose are vital in ensuring that values and purpose remain at the forefront of individuals' minds.

Imagine a non-profit organization dedicated to promoting environmental conservation and sustainability. The organization's mission is to protect endangered species and preserve natural habitats. To ensure that the values and purpose of the organization remain at the forefront of its members' minds, the leaders employ effective communication strategies and consistent reinforcement.

During regular team meetings, the executive director and other leaders take the opportunity to emphasize the organization's core values and its long-term vision. They share success stories of how their efforts have made a positive impact on endangered species and ecosystems, illustrating the direct link between their work and the organization's purpose.

Moreover, the organization leverages various communication channels to keep members informed and engaged. They maintain an internal communication platform where updates and relevant environmental news are regularly shared. This platform also allows team members to exchange ideas and provide feedback.

Aligning values and purpose inspires and motivates individuals by connecting their personal goals to the organization's mission. When individuals see that their goals and values align with those of the organization, they feel a deeper sense of purpose and fulfillment in their work.

The profound influence of empathy in leadership serves as a dynamic force that not only shapes organizational cultures but also drives exceptional results. Through a comprehensive understanding of the dynamics of empathy, leaders embark on a journey that encompasses numerous aspects, each contributing to the overall effectiveness of their leadership approach.

Effective communication and active listening skills become vital tools that empower leaders to inspire teamwork and foster a sense of unity. The empathetic leader's ability to truly hear and understand the perspectives of others translates into meaningful dialogue, where ideas are freely exchanged and collective creativity flourishes.

Sustainable and high-performing teams emerge as the natural outcome of empathetic leadership. By nurturing a culture of collaboration, respect, and understanding, leaders create an environment where individuals are empowered to exceed expectations and contribute their best efforts.

Finally, the alignment of values and purpose solidifies the foundation for success, uniting individuals around a shared vision that inspires commitment and determination. This alignment becomes the compass that guides actions and decisions, ensuring that every endeavor contributes to the collective journey toward exceptional results.

In essence, the integration of empathy across these dimensions creates a harmonious symphony of leadership excellence. It is a journey that celebrates self-awareness, trust, communication, resilience, empowerment, conflict resolution, team performance, and shared purpose – all harmonizing together to orchestrate the triumphant crescendo of exceptional leadership and organizational success.

Aligning Values with Purpose Worksheet

Step 1: Identify Your Core Values

List your top core values. These are the principles that guide your decisions, actions, and behavior. Choose the values that resonate most with you.

- Value 1:
- Value 2:
- Value 3:

Step 2: Reflect on Your Purpose

Consider your personal or team purpose. This is the reason why you do what you do. Reflect on how your actions align with your core values.

- Purpose Statement: [Write a concise statement that captures your personal or team purpose.]
- How Does Your Purpose Align with Your Core Values?
  - Value 1 - 3: How does your purpose support or embody this value?

Step 3: Setting Aligned Goals

List specific goals or actions that align your purpose with your core values. These goals should reflect your commitment to living and working in accordance with what matters most to you.

- Aligned Goals 1 - 3:
  - Description: [Describe the goal that aligns with your purpose and value.]
  - Timeline: [Set a realistic timeline for achieving this goal.]
  - Action Steps: [List the steps you need to take to reach this goal.]

Step 4: Reflection and Adaptation

Regularly reflect on your progress in aligning your values with your purpose:

- How have your values influenced your decisions and actions?
- Are there any challenges or setbacks you've encountered? How did you overcome them?
- Have you experienced any moments of alignment that have been particularly meaningful?

Step 5: Next Steps

Plan for continuous alignment:
- How will you continue to integrate your values into your purposeful actions?
- Are there any adjustments or new goals you need to set to maintain alignment?
- How will you ensure that your actions consistently reflect your core values and purpose?

www.ingramcontent.com/pod-product-compliance
Lightning Source LLC
Chambersburg PA
CBHW062349290526
45794CB00005B/2153